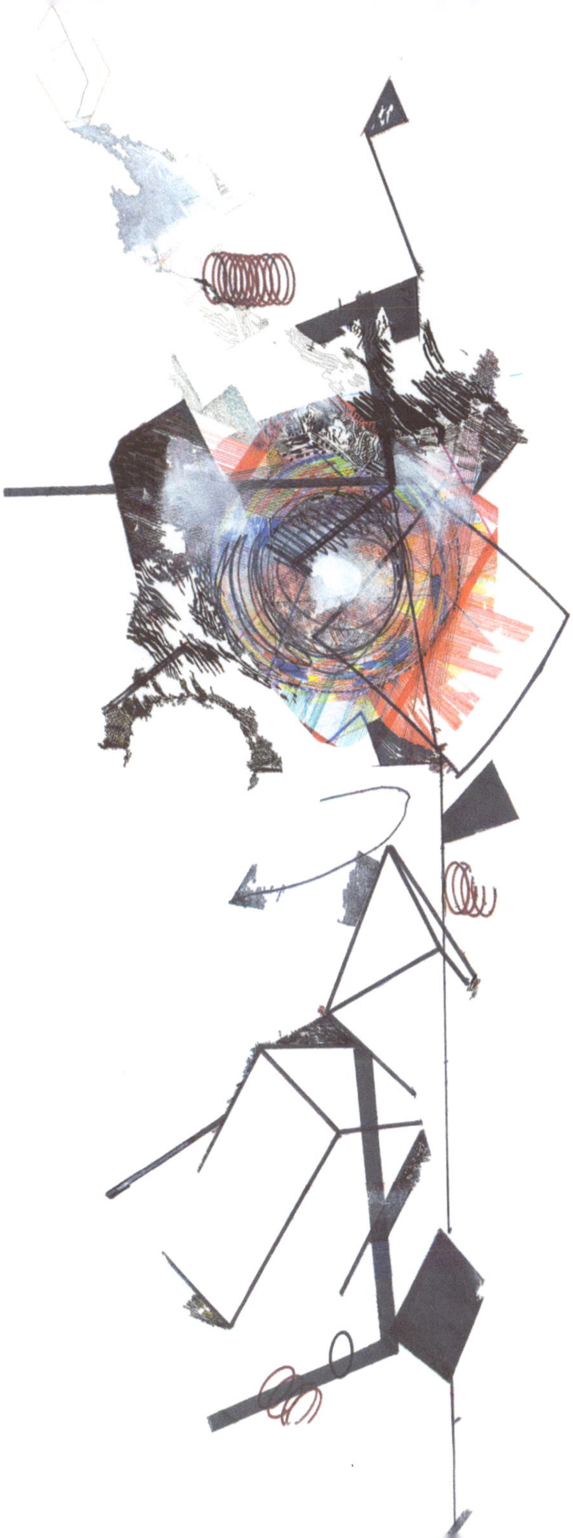

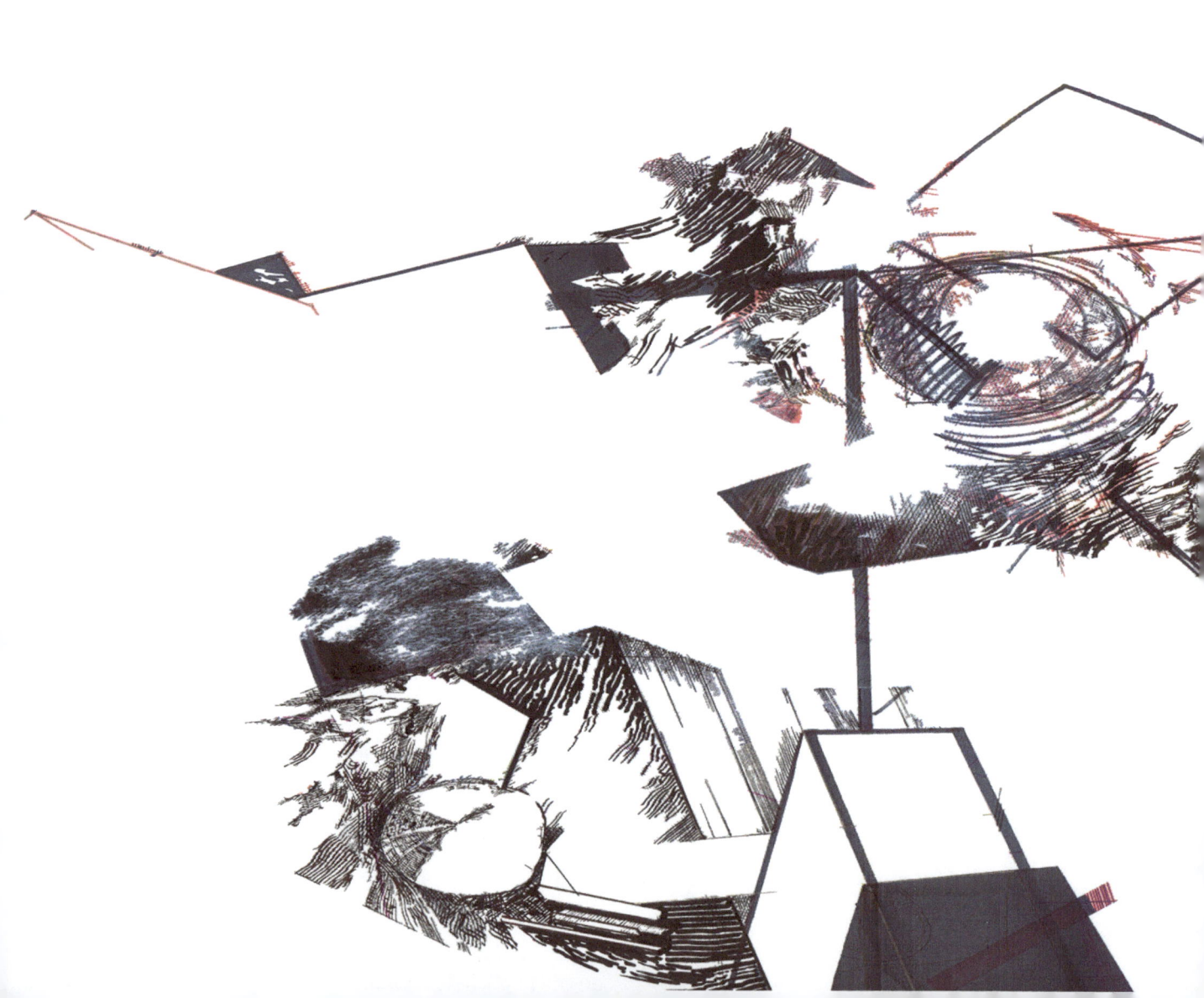

poems by
hugh merrill

Stubborn Mule Press
Devil's Elbow, MO
stubbornmulepress.com

Copyright (c) Hugh Merrill, 2018
First Edition 11 7 5 3 2 1
ISBN: 978-1-946642-72-1
Library of Congress Control Number: 2018910965

Design, edits and layout: Jeanette Powers
stubbornmulepress@gmail.com
All Artwork: Hugh Merrill

All rights reserved. No part of this publication may be reproduced or transmitted in any form or by any means, electronic or mechanical, including photocopying, recording or by info retrieval system, w/out prior written permission from the author.

Also by Hugh Merrill
    Nomadic: Rover by Days Singing These Gang Plank Songs of the Ambler (39 West Press, 2016)
contact: hughmerr@hotmail.com

*Tell him it's crucial to know
if in truth this is brotherly love. He won't
get angry, he's too tired for anger,
too relieved to be here, he won't even laugh
though he'll find you silly.*

--from **An Extraordinary Morning** by Philip Levine

to Philip Levine
& all who have this courage
to give a voice for the voiceless
a voice for themselves

HM

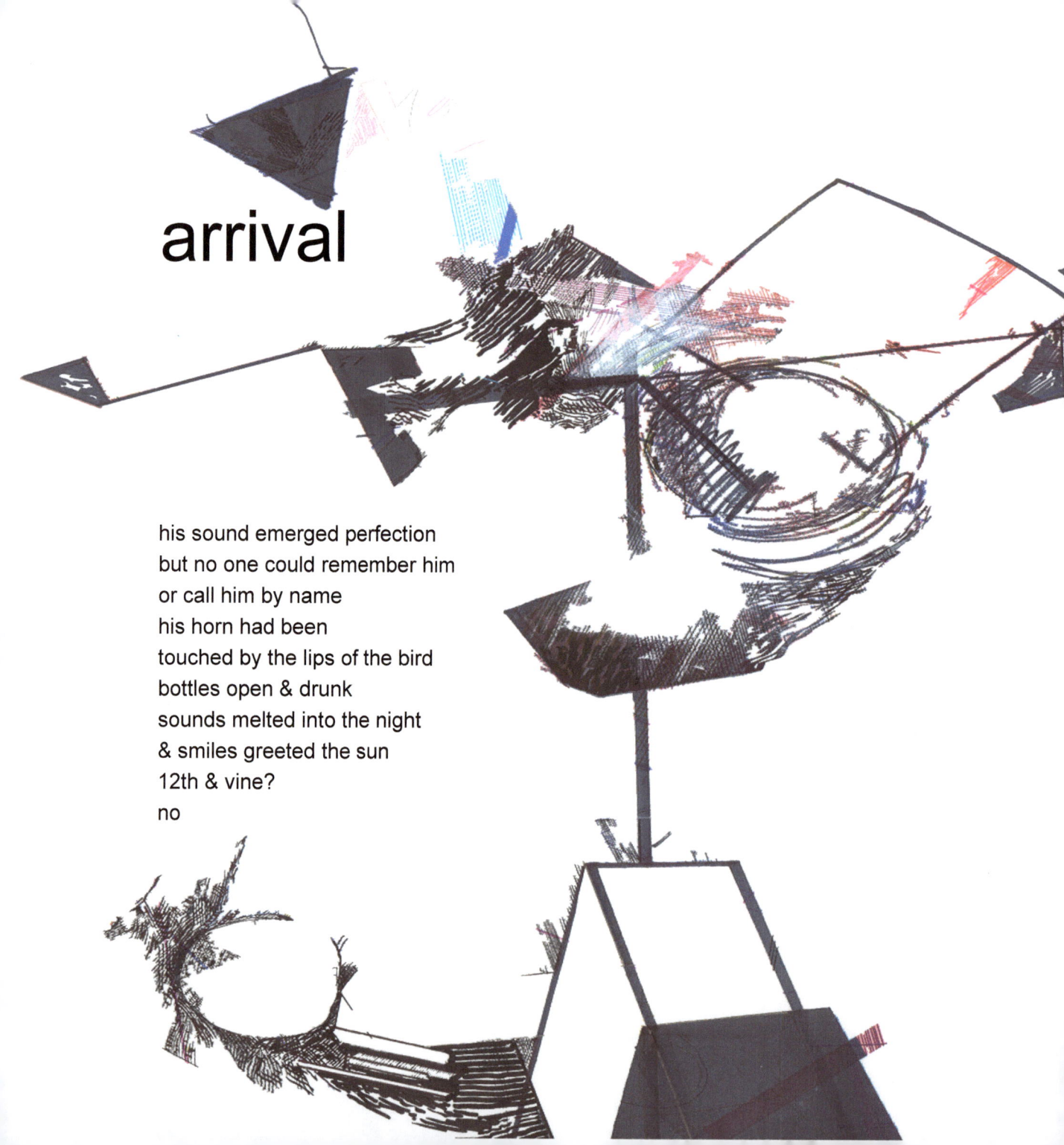

arrival

his sound emerged perfection
but no one could remember him
or call him by name
his horn had been
touched by the lips of the bird
bottles open & drunk
sounds melted into the night
& smiles greeted the sun
12th & vine?
no

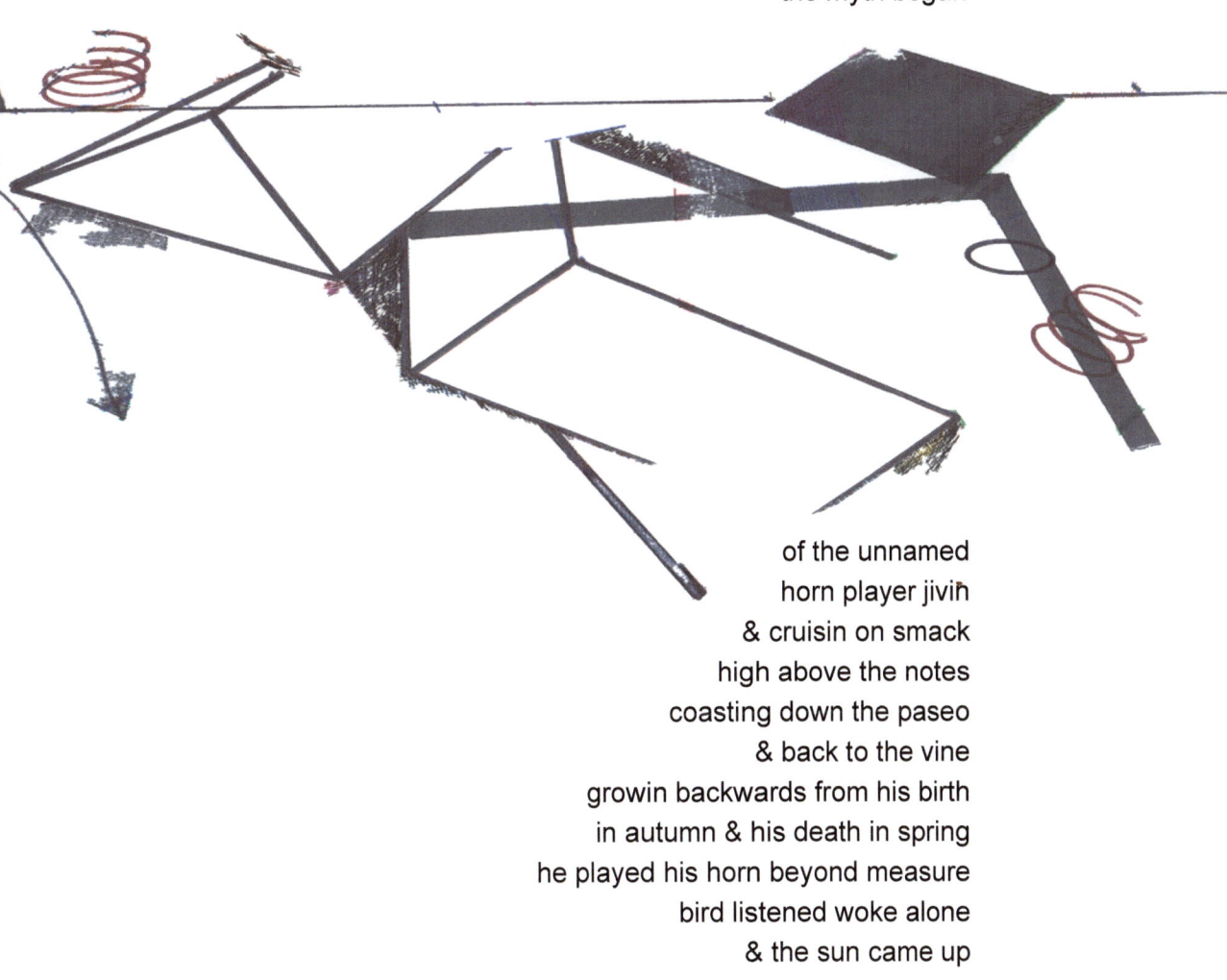

dylan told me nothin's standin there
go east further east
to some unknown address
the myth began

of the unnamed
horn player jivin
& cruisin on smack
high above the notes
coasting down the paseo
& back to the vine
growin backwards from his birth
in autumn & his death in spring
he played his horn beyond measure
bird listened woke alone
& the sun came up

the volkswagen
a 1972
spread toward the river city
the prairie city
the fm radio blared
out a story of cows
steers loose on main street
open windows
the speed
the air relieved the heat
of early june
hot
but it aint so bad it aint so bad
& mike murphy's cattle drive
had gone berserk
the steers would not play their part
crashed through
wooden street barriers
roamed up 12th street
going to city hall
others headed
west to the majestic for a beer
no no no
they wanted scotch
& a big cigar
a few turned right
headed east into a parking garage
marching up the ramps

single mindedly
there in the weed trees
behind the musicians foundation
are the remains of a bed
& box springs
thrown out in 1956
ella slept with her rusty drummer
they made those springs dance
an unmatched performance
such timing & percussion
a beat never accomplished before
the mystery horn player
blew to their rhythm
the rhythm of the dancing box springs
blowing infinite lines of scat
the horn was joined by the scream
of a wounded one eyed alley cat
the next day
someone dragged the mattress springs
& bed into the alley behind the foundation
slept naked on those box springs at night
blowing bebop to the trees all day
mmmmmmmm
bebop
be
bop
bebob
bbbbobobobobo

• • •

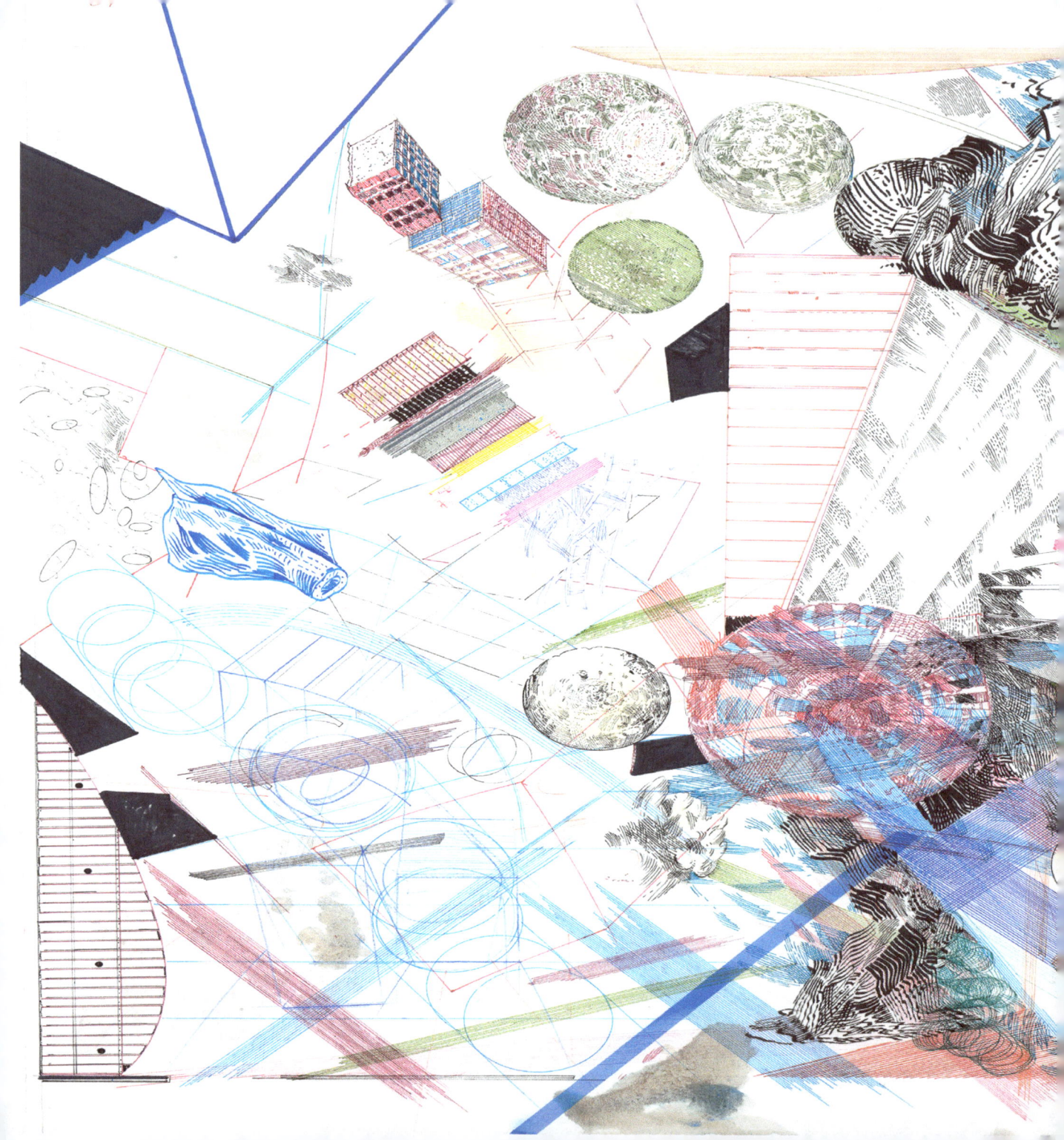

until the whiskey ran out
the steers reached the top
of the garage
the 6th level
& there was no place to go but heaven
the vw edged
closer to the city
& the driver leaned forward
listened to the radio report on the wayward cattle
the wind whipped through the open window
they shot the damn cows
he screamed
fuck they shot the damn cows
reporter said
they could not get them to go down the ramp
so
so they shot the damn cows
the vw
entered the city limits
saw the skyline
with its setting summer sun
somewhere in the view was the garage
filled with shot dead cows
cows now
being dragged by a chain
with a pickup truck
the bones of the bed springs
far outlasted the bones of the cows

her search for anaïs nin

she lay on top of him
& her legs spread

searching deep in
herself for climax

like a journal page
or camera she examines

herself
wanting to record all

know it all
physically

& intellectually
his penis enters her

they become a singularity
& remain a duality

a contradiction
& an oxymoron

her body saturates his body
his lives well lived

balance her distance
her worlds of sexual passion

her desires are a novel
becoming

she wants all of him
she wanted to be

from him
in him

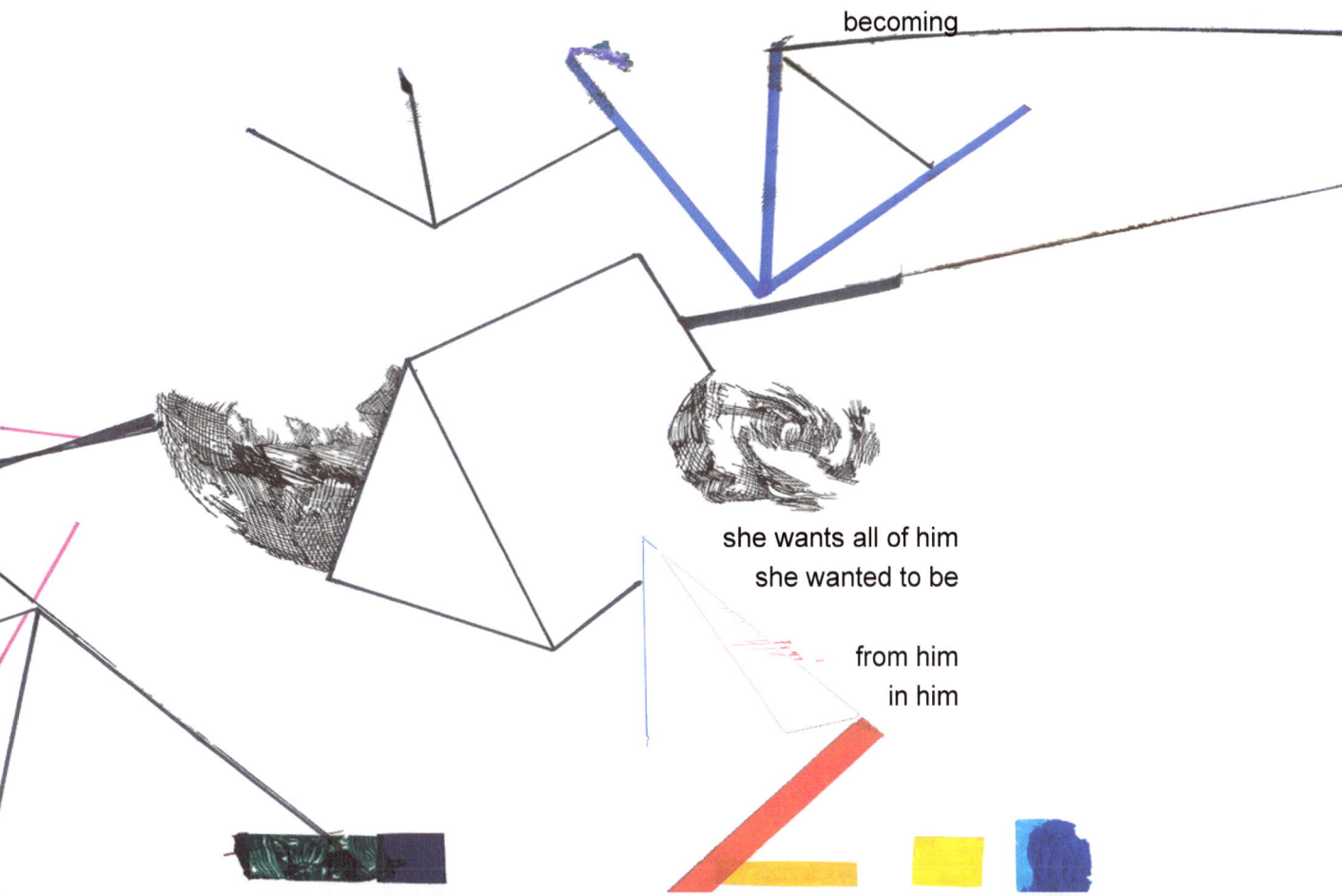

    of him
    & through him

                                she fucks him
                                & acquires essences

        of times long past
        loves long lost

                                she arrests him
                                & makes him

new
  k n o w

                                    new
                              as she is new

        & knows
        & is growing

                                inside
                                intuitively
      instinctually
      & emotionally

                          she knows
                          & needs his phantom
        ghost
        lives
              to be coursing through
                            her
          through her
          pumping
                  arterial
                aspiration

a night in—
in the wind & the rain

rosemary the girl hiding behind the cloud of pot
said her father runs screaming about
crimes she committed
she lost her virginity to a sailor at twelve
lost it again at twenty-one
the old dean whispered
from the women's room
rose is in the truck stop

just for fun
she hitched a ride
& is hiding a gun

she ends up killing the ghosts on route 491
killing the ghosts of blues players
& fiddlers
same sad victims each time
leaving only silence
at the crossroads
& broken bottles of corn rye

. . .

these sponges of time have dry bones
& a toasted ass light the long coon's tail
but in the wind you can hear the ocean whale

she inhaled his seeds
saw jesus in a rust stain
stole the same car three times
then broke down in front of the
velvet moon

darryl said *get in*

picked up
& driven to the edge of town
had his baby
a trans boy with the roma eyes
born with an erection

& his mind is gristle
he worships an implied sun
lives the monk's life
feeds rabbits hides in storm drains
& will someday divorce

herself

meat patrol

wading through petrol
the desert tortoises drown
near the groping lovers
where broken hearted clerics weep
in the temple's cocoon the choir whispered

i do not understand these bodies

no one heard their song
or the bleating of abe's dead sheep
the mob found a place that fosters
no bias except money
& race
& the rest of time
they butchered the wailing poets on the killing room floor
their skins were covered in severed signatures
not a stitch more
the tattoo artist is to blame
each got a number not a name
when they arrived
they found only death
(no start again)
it always came out the same

when the empress moved

she had lost her glow
moved away shut down
i had returned

i had returned
to see the remnants
of the faded red lettering
in fake chinese/english
script

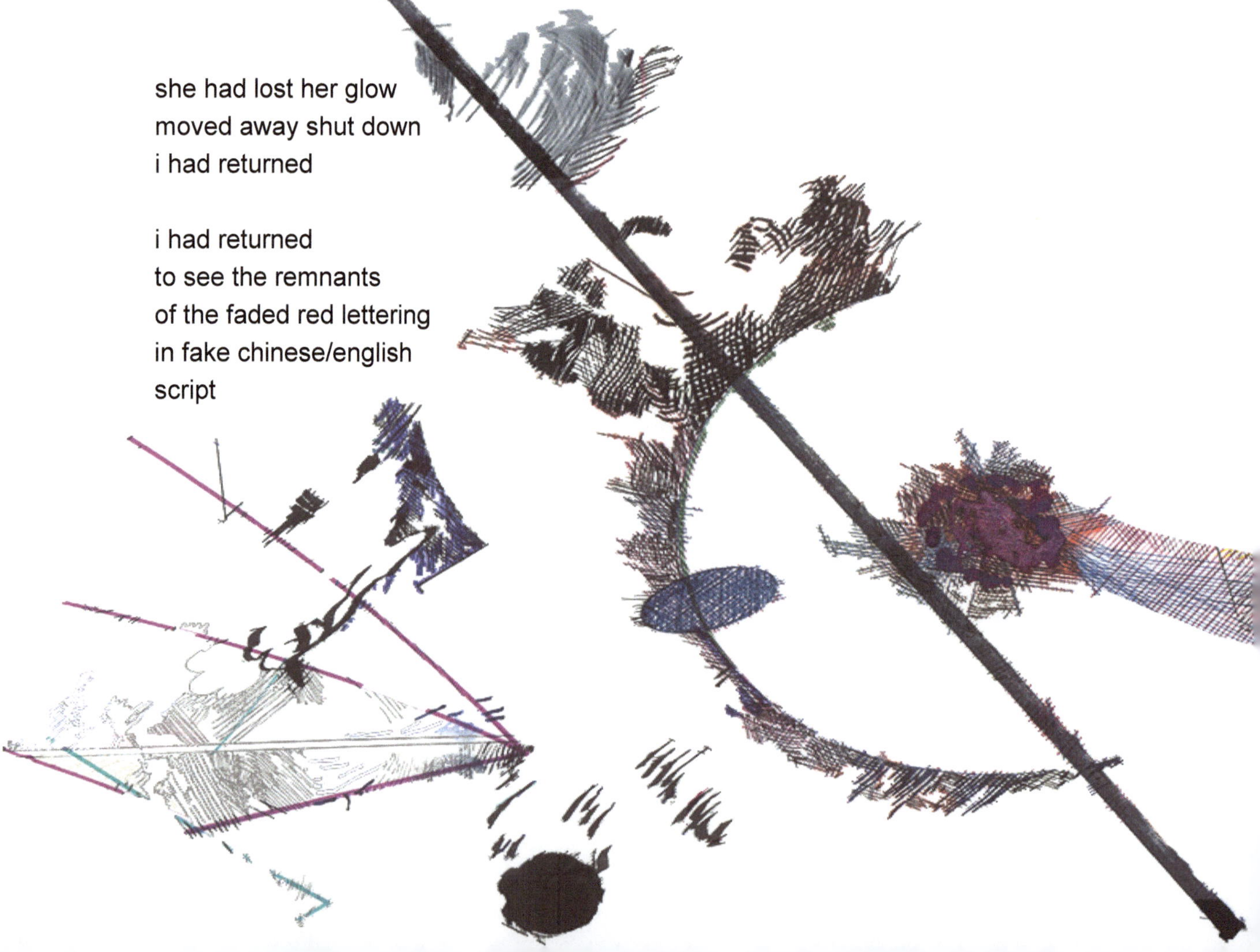

the chinese empress
a restaurant once shiny
& new
neon outlined now busted down
broken glass an empty storefront
she had lost her glow

i had dinner there with a roma
in 1973 or was it 4
she came to my table
in the darkness of winter
perfumed with natural oils
& essentials she
ordered bowls of fish soup
& noodles for us
i ate in silence she told me her life story
married to a marine lost her son
& family

stories of rough times
she happily described
in detail how to mix love potion no 9
i took notes on a napkin
but forgot it as we left together

night

night

the sun came up
i saw the empty needle on her
bathroom floor the leather strap by the toilet
tried to wake her but she was deep in the nod
she had not described her world as a junkie
but i was not surprised the rug was stained

& damp

i put on my socks
the cats hid under the bed
happy in their magical room of junk
i left stepping over theatrical costumes
half-filled bottles of oils

& perfumes

beer bottles & empty chinese takeout boxes
i vaguely remember the long walk from her apartment
on north avenue to the tavern most likely searching
for a hangover cure a cheeseburger
still searching i guess

the baltimore grey december wind
shook me from those memories
i nodded at myself in the broken glass window
& thought
the chinese empress has moved on long ago

dog alley

two white trash kids white trash kids living in the hood
someplace south of north ave perhaps on green street
dangerous place night or day black or white
                                           dangerous place
i caught i caught their latest act an act of hatred
& violence of stupidity they beat down
the half-starved neighborhood dog

she was a black dog
roamed the alleys near maryland ave
the black dog was was left
in a bloody sweat soaked puddle of pain
the boys stood laughing near the blossoming wisteria
in the alley running behind the greek orthodox church
the alley just across from my third floor fire escape
window oddly permanently painted shut perhaps
for decades i saw the boys turn
& walk off laughing
the dog the dog she lay lifeless no one interfered
those those waiting at the bus stop shook their heads
talked loudly gestured one old man on the corner yelled
                                                 but no one tried to stop them

                                     i went back to work on my drawing

laid out on the wooden table
the only piece of furniture
in the small room
listened to dylan
became lost became lost in my thoughts
in late late afternoon i noticed
someone had placed a flowering branch
ripped from the pear tree in the church yard
over the carcass a fierce spring snow fell
big wet flakes

later as i walked past on my way to dinner
at the chinese empress the evening's twilight reflected
off the dog's black coat
revealing traces traces of purple
green on blood red snow
the tones of a spring day so blinding
the bright yellow greens now
subdued mixing quickly
with sadder darker blue/violet
shades
dog wisteria
pear branch
flowers garbage
a broken broom handle
all all magically retreating
into the consuming darkness
of night

in spring at dawn it is most beautiful

in spring at dawn it is most beautiful
even for those sleeping behind the dumpster
you i go to work on the early bus

we see them rise from their tombs
shake off the night's cold shuffle through their
numerous pockets in coats too heavy

for the coming warmth of this april day
but no no no no not warm enough
for the cold misty night ahead

wine helps god's orange light
silhouettes the buildings faint brusies
of purple are turning toward yellow

it is the race of changing colors
& forms most beautiful
we do not know each other

only nod
identification at the bus stop
in spring at dawn it is most beautiful

italian clown's head

hacking against the monster
they all disappeared under the flow of waves
where every space filled with life's small trinkets
saving no air for the living this river of
commerce turning corners
& making
electric poles into ships' masts
then mere logs joining the rising tide of pain
& debris

the monster ebbs
in fields miles from the coast then sucks back
all the world's crap pushed flows forward
now sucked back toward a nocturnal tomb
this ocean's river pulls apart a doll
an italian clown dressed in silk smiling
then a separated arm then goes the articulated legs
leaving only the decapitated yet smiling head
purchased in florence
flown to a prefecture in japan
swept away with her family
on a radioactive tide of garbage
the italian clown's head
bobs in the vast current of

destruction now headed forever east the smiling
head of the italian clown headed forever east
driven to the bottom by unmeasured currents
a mile deep where darkness sand
& dirt are invisible

the sea monster holding
the smiling clown's head in its crushing gravity
the italian clown smiling in darkness
smiling in the realm with no light
no reflection only night's deepest shadows
here the italian clown's smiling face
bounces across barren sand
& mud flats
passes fluorescent forms swimming deeply
to rise to rise slowly passing diving blue whales
in search of giant squids smiling italian clown
is carried by currents floating like a meditating disciple
thousands of miles waiting for a glimpse of the sun
the head of the smiling italian clown crosses
the tidal shelf is imprisoned in kelp beds is freed
& is tumbled toward shore
smashed against rocks swept down an estuary
is inspected by sea lions the italian clown
its smiling face up at last on stage
swirled into a pool of starfish barnacles urchins
& anemones
perhaps at last home in the circus of the sea

different ways of speaking

the sweet language the idiom of the rat digital lips data revealing no information brother owns the banker's wife's moist dew fat baby looking for queen jane wearing frocks in stratford hall the smell of mildew yellowish perfume natural victory merely growing old the linger language barren smiles of the portrait gallery 4 am nodding at the wall seabirds demonic & green the voice of the other you knew speaking in different ways

yes
in different ways

trickster games

in our general state of putrefaction
we are left sipping a distilled ear of corn
with its fiery nature
homemade clear intensified
setting off philosophical quicksilver
& transforming our intellect to mythology
releasing unremembered fairy-tale poems of despair

hermes arrived late
but she had already scouted out the serpent's mating dance with coyote
copulating in the window of a skyscraper far away on another continent
athena did not even look up or   cum
comebuy you   my black slave of delight
cumbuy me? white boys for sale on la streets

then an unnamed buddha from an immaterial universe
cuts through time relations space
& timber
cutting through the mythic
& the real
cutting through perception
invited none of that bullshit to exist

loki with his lips sewn shut

hummed
& spit
slammed
& hammered
the song of the dying forge

no more than a split steam a lackawanna
a stream of piss
& fire perhaps
a lost language in wilkes-barre
where anthracite glowed alive
on the factory floor
until its certain death
november 4 1980

oh centro american mythical deer dancing monster
let go my tail wait i hear the roadhouse blues
& the guitar playing at the crossroads
jim is there
or is it those tricksters flying about till dawn
last night they make a life new for everyone
sunrises
& the flickering traces
of their trickster games fade into sparks
like kanefusa's steel blades cutting all materials

like butter baby
it's just like cutting butter

observations

quick step two step from texas to carolina the guitars wail

the old toad hated the rain but kept a steady course
drowning in the sand bunker of the 16th hole
anniston alabama country club 1957

in the woods was the remnant of his 6 iron bent
& thrown there over 50 years ago
during the club championship

downtown the black preacher dressed sharp
& never stopping her commentaries
by her account forgiving was easier than being forgiven

forgiving you left something for the other
receiving forgiveness you had a gift you could not return
we're not sure how it operates

there are no instructions
the preacher laughed shook her finger pointed toward heaven
mississippi god damn alabama got me so upset!

the choir sang quick quick thank you nina thank you

summer wind

(act i)

the morning star
but a dream
i hear the rain pouring in
hear it splatter?
here it splatters on the crust of the mexican desert
it's a bloody torrent a squall

no------this heavy rain
pours from the speaker of my iphone
pandora's ambient noises fill the room
reaching out across the barren parking lot
into our vast wasteland of parked cars
eternal internal
& below

the early morning's summer heat
rises through shaded windows
recalling last night's whining joy
its mojitos
& tequilas
its lust
& pleasures

leaving grinning idiots
fingering the dampness
of a mercurial cum shot

a broken swamp cooler
suffering a breeze that cools nothing
not the imagination certainly not my heart

beating beating beating

above your sleeping silence

(act ii)

we tumble we tumble we tumble
vacationers argue in the parking lot
we tumble into the sheets
we tumble with the freedom of falling into a wave
we tumble having no substance
we tumble without weight
we tumble without
without

light sound wind birds
traffic touch smell names
histories love we tumble

        we tumble

      undefined ----- we tumble
        in a country of old men
      we tumble tumble we tumble
        in our own magnificence
forever mirrored in a sexual dance we tumble

     the door slams frighten grasping
        deep inside each other
   together we remain silent holding tight
     then filled with laughter we tumble

        the trickster has returned
    the summer's wind changes all

on doing the wash

she worked full time as a secretary
the trembling of the river
musically lifting a branch from the shoreline
my lover came in to hover over me

drifting rain losing the light of day howling
& there goes the cell phone
buzzing like the vibrator's joy
small birds scream confused the cat?

or just the smell of burning rubbish
richard enters the office looking like a sailor proud of his ship
the earth stretches like a black sea hiding stories a century old
i am middle class went to a suburban high school colors were blue

& gold the sea birds grey dancing at the edge of foam
& sand god i went through thick to thin to get this audition
the ocean's roaring call the gentle lion the dark faltering pines
i lift my dirty panties drop them into the washing machine

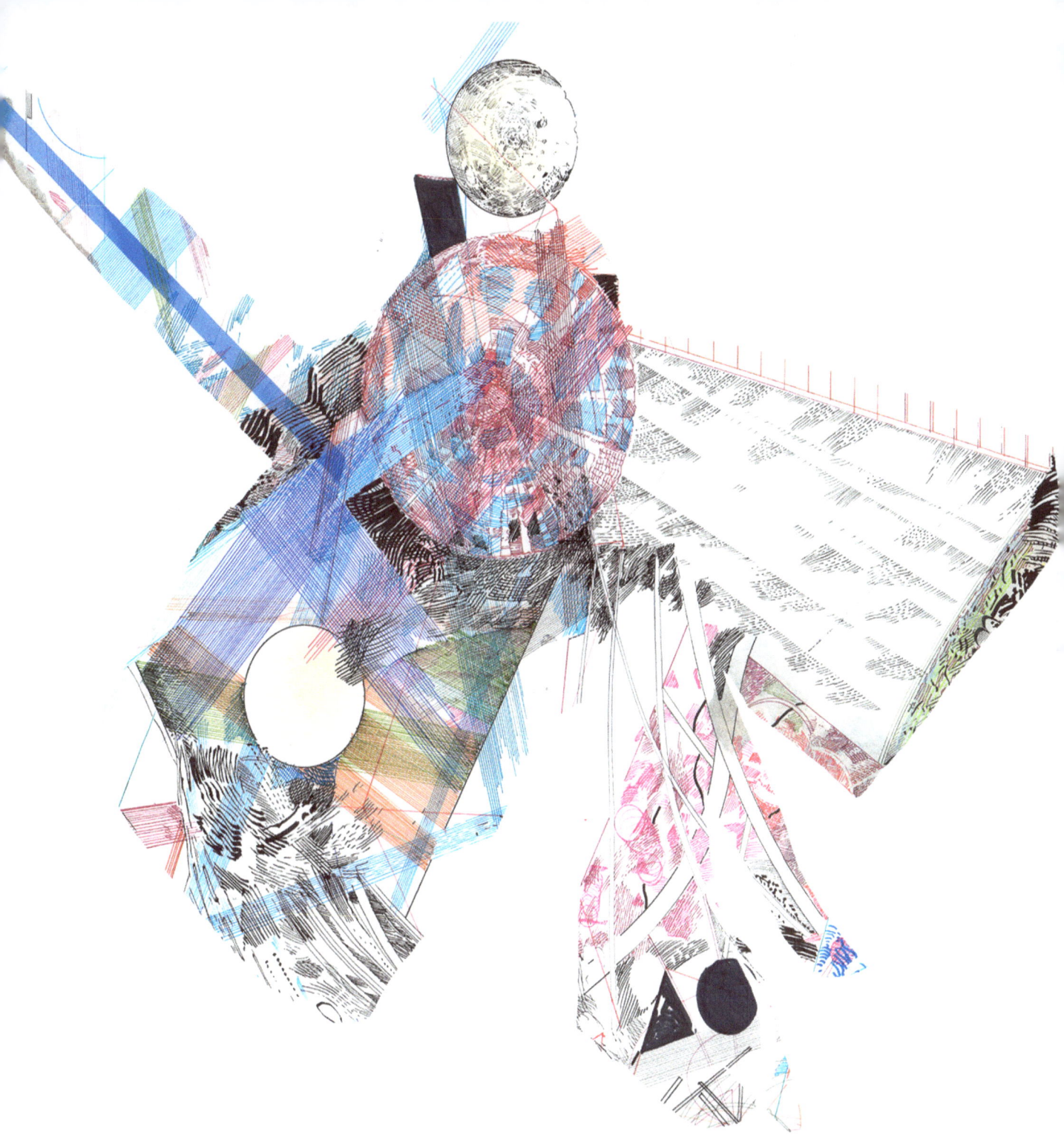

heritage

her mother's eerie
& sinister giggles floated in the front seat
her jeans are off
& her legs spread
with crayon in hand
martha sees only her mother's feet
hovering above with red painted toe nails
feet pushing against the roof
of the abandoned chevy
mom
& lee moaning
sounding like the mating grunts of feral pigs

outside
prints from real hog hooves
embossed in the red clay
lead to the car door long ago ripped off
& now lying in the creek 100 yards away
martha follows
the prints to the creek
making her mark in the soft clay

the monuments to the fortunate
are in the country club parking lot

18 holes of trent jones golf beautiful fairways
& drinks before during
& after
the friendly match

the kind words
& the civilized manner
confederate toy soldiers
marching home on a persian rug

it's not hate it's heritage they repeat
things had to change but it should not
have happened the way it did
the confederate flag
a battle flag
painted on the hood of his ford truck
two flying above the truck bed
no need for the federal government to have...
he goes on
& on
repeating the old myths
his daughter working the dixie mart
carries a gun on her belt just in case

martha with her mom
& lee appear from the edge of the woods laughing
& dancing across the emerald green cow pasture
home heading home

in tears

in tears of remembrance
the land of dreams begins
my souls are carried by twilight's sky
forming clouds of what seemed to have been mine
now all changed
& gone
the wind dries your saltwater tears
before they can soothe my thirst
the rain does not reach the desert floor
here all remains dry
& dead
grim reaper shouting
in different languages
we cannot understand
this is the sunset of memory
leaving all of us in solitude
alone
end the end
to become one
within
the
nocturnal
cycle
of
morning
mourning
& becoming

eurydice

i have seen you from my window
in twilight you were there
in those moments you were mine

my clothes the dirty sheets lay curled up like a pet
i fall into a world without you
the party of that evening now distant as the mountains

all that humid night illuminated by a single incandescent bulb
we were grasping for a piece of the moon
burning like the reflection of a sunrise between our hands

no one saw your happy soul recede
turn into a clenched fist suddenly leaving
who else are you who else is there

why will love come
& go so suddenly
i feel you are far away

always daybreak erasing
your ghost
twilight?
i search for you again

www.ingramcontent.com/pod-product-compliance
Lightning Source LLC
Chambersburg PA
CBHW050736110526
44591CB00003B/40